"Read Your Lover's Environment Like a Book!"

"This deeply insightful book belongs in every woman's library. Helen Arabanos opens your Feng Shui eyes so that you can read a lover's environment like a book! Now you will know how to clearly interpret what you are seeing and feeling and make wise choices in your romantic relationships."

-TERAH KATHRYN COLLINS, Best-selling author of
The Western Guide to Feng Shui

"A Terrific and Insightful Read."

"Can you actually discover if you will be compatible with someone by the art on his wall or where his television is placed? The surprising answer is revealed in Helen Arabanos' book *He's Into You...But Is His home?* Taking us into the world of "interpersonal Feng Shui," Helen shows how our relationships are affected by these subtle and not-so-subtle cues. It also helps us understand that which we can affect and that which we cannot, when it comes to relationships and compatibility. A terrific and insightful read."

-STEVE VOLLUM, Business Entrepreneur, Inventor and Engineer
Inventor of the *Fortune Compass*,
The world's first electronic Feng Shui Compass

"Get a Clue Before It's Too Late!!"

"Your thoughts and beliefs about yourself and your life are reflected in your choices. Your style of dress, the kind of car you drive and your living environment are all outward expressions of your subconscious mind. *He's Into You...But Is His home?* clearly illustrates how a peek into someone's home tells much about the occupant's beliefs, needs and wants. With wit and insight, Helen Arabanos has succeeded in showing us how the ancient art of Feng Shui is a 21st Century tool for looking into our relationships. *He's Into You...But Is His home?* is a must read for any woman who wants some clue about what she's getting into before it's too late!!"

- PATRICIA LYNN BELKOWITZ, C.Ht., EFT-CC, Clinical
Hypnotherapist and author of
TheMindMatters Manifestation Manual and *Erotica~101*

HE'S INTO YOU...

But Is His Home?

What a Man's Feng Shui Can Reveal About Him

Helen Arabanos

Full Bloom Feng Shui

He's Into You...But Is His Home?

From the *Walls Do Talk* Series

For more information:
Full Bloom Feng Shui
1014 S. Westlake Boulevard, #14-289
Westlake Village, CA 91361

www.FullBloomFengShui.com

ISBN: **978-0615489001**

First Edition published 2011
Second Edition published 2011

Printed in the United States of America

To Women Everywhere

May you find the man you want, and recognize when he's in front of you and when he's not.

Preface

Where to Begin

So you think he's wonderful. You've already started envisioning your future with him. And yet, you aren't certain he feels the same, or it's not moving forward as quickly as you'd like, or.... This book will help you sort out which doubts you need to pay attention to and which doubts can be alleviated.

This book contains several "how to" tips but I don't advise your jumping in and suggesting them to the object of your affection all at once. Step back, pace yourself, and be ready to open your eyes. Observe, analyze and then take action. That may mean slowing things down or making a few suggestions, or maybe deciding it is time to look for a new relationship. The right action depends upon your observations, your commitments, and of course, his willingness to participate in making changes to his living space/home.

I recommend that you read through each section and make note of each point that applies to your prospective mate's home, or to your own home. You'll find pages for notes throughout. Remember it's about balance. A few check marks don't mean you should turn and run, but a lot of check marks may be telling you that is exactly what you need to do!

Acknowledgment

They say "it takes a village" and this book certainly did. With love and gratitude, I thank you all.

Sue, you are an Angel.

My clients, whether your story was included here or not, you have been a part of this. I learn from you just as I share my knowledge and experience with you. It was through having the pleasure of meeting you that this book came to be and that others will learn.

James, Michael and Harry, thank you for all of your guidance.

Patricia, Erna, Lori, Dede, Scott, Demmica, Ed, Candice, Diane, Christian, Claudina, Lisa, Michael, Terah, Steve, and Johnny, thank you for your contributions.

Gratitude for my many teachers who have taught me about Feng Shui, energy, healing, men, relationships and life.

My friends, for your love, support and encouragement. You inspire and amaze me.

My family, who taught me how important a peaceful home environment is and that Feng Shui will help create one.

Introduction

First there was *The Rules*; then came *He's Just Not That Into You* and now *The Walls Do Talk*. This book gives you access to understanding what he (or she) is attracting into his life by looking at the space he lives in. Regardless of what he tells you, if his house says something different, the relationship is likely to have challenges and a favorable outcome could be elusive.

WINSTON CHURCHILL

"We shape our buildings; thereafter they shape us."

This book is designed to help you read between the lines, or the walls, as the case may be. Although it is based on Feng Shui philosophies, it is not the typical Feng Shui "how to" book. Its intention is to help you look at a space using Feng Shui Principles; enabling you to learn about the person who occupies that space and, by the nature of his living environment, what he is allowing into his life. It shows you how to interpret a person's home as a reflection of his head and heart.

Although the masculine pronoun form has been used throughout this book, the information can be applied to anyone's home, male or female, to gain a better understanding of them and their current relationship potential. So whatever your sexual preference, this book will give you insight into the man or woman with whom you are seeking an intimate connection.

And of course, there are "how to" tips that you can suggest to your prospective partner. His willingness to make the changes you suggest will also give you insight into his willingness to move forward with the relationship.

Don't forget to look around your own home and apply what you learn in this book to your living space to make sure that *your* environment is ready for the relationship you say you want.

HE'S INTO YOU...

But Is His Home?

What a Man's Feng Shui Can Reveal About Him

His Foyer/Entry

The entry way of a home gives the first impression. In Feng Shui, we refer to the entrance of a property as "the mouth of Chi" – the place that energy enters and leaves a structure. It is one of the three most important areas of a home. It is the spot where guests are welcomed and where they are sent safely on their way. It is the first impression and also how something is remembered.

What does the entrance to his home tell you about him and the direction your relationship may go? If you can pass through the entrance without any hindrance or distraction, he's telling you that you are welcome to join him. He is freely and easily inviting you into his home, his space, and possibly his life. He wants to provide easy access. He's open, welcome, inviting, and quite possibly ready for what you are looking for.

If you have to step over or maneuver around obstacles, then perhaps he's telling you that that you can visit, but he doesn't want you to plan on staying. He likely has excuses for this obstacle course: "I travel a lot for work," "I'd rather do other things with my time than clean," "I need a bigger place," "I just got home and had to walk my dog before you got here and I didn't have time to put my things away," or any other explanation for the items that have taken up residency in the entry of his home.

Of course, if the next time you are invited over, you are greeted with the same obstacle course and similar excuses, it's likely that this is the way he lives and he's making it clear that he puts in blocks; physical blocks and possibly emotional blocks as well.

MOUTH OF CHI

The mouth of Chi is used to refer to the point where energy enters. Just as food enters your mouth, energy enters a home through an opening, most often the front door.

In Feng Shui, the first thing seen when entering a space is the "Greeter." The Greeter sends a message to an arriving guest. It is a positive sign if it is a lush plant, a lovely sculpture, a beautiful piece of art, an inviting place to sit, or a welcome mat.

What is the first thing you notice when you walk in? Don't dismiss it; take special note of it. That first item, in Feng Shui terms, is his Greeter and it is sending you a loud and clear message about him, his life, his view and what he wants you to think of him. Are you greeted by his baseball bat, his snowboard, or his golf clubs? Or perhaps you're greeted by his guitar, his briefcase, or his toolbox? Do *you* keep your yoga mat or your ballet slippers or your sewing machine at your front door? If so, like him, you are saying the other person will have to work around those other things. These things include pet paraphernalia. If his entry is crowded with kitty litter boxes, dog beds, leashes or toys, then a well-loved pet may have precedence over you and your relationship.

GREETER

In Feng Shui, the first thing seen when entering a space is the Greeter. You want to be intentional with this. Choose something that conveys the message you want for your arriving guests, whether that's a lush plant, a lovely sculpture, a beautiful piece of art, an inviting place to sit or a welcome mat.

Don't forget to take into account the frequency with which he invites you over. I was working with a woman recently who was excited because her boyfriend of over one year had just invited her to his house for the first time. An entire YEAR! And she was excited and happy! Why hadn't he invited her over sooner? The why doesn't really matter. Is there any explanation for this that would make you feel cherished, loved and welcomed into his life? There are none that I can think of. That doesn't mean there aren't any. You need to think carefully about his behavior and see if his behavior fits into your goals, desires, and timeframe.

4

One woman told me how the man she had been dating had invited her to his home for the first time after dating for several months. It was late at night and seemed to be an invitation to come over for sex. She asked why he hadn't previously invited her over. He said that he was embarrassed for her to see how he lived.

If you hear something like that, take heed! If his home isn't ready for you, chances are he isn't ready for you either and he's telling you that loud and clear! Before you write him off though, watch what he does next. Does he begin taking actions to prepare his space for you? If so, you may not want to give up on him or the potential for this relationship.

The man who made that late night invitation, got into action shortly after that conversation. He changed jobs and moved to a much nicer place, to which he invited her to right away. Soon after that he bought a new home to which she was also invited.

If a man is interested in a woman, he wants to impress her. He wants to show her what he has to offer her. Take a look around. What kind of first impression is he giving you through the entrance to his home? Take careful note of that. It will give you an idea of how hard he's willing to work to earn your time and affection.

One additional comment, if he thinks his home isn't up to the level he thinks you deserve, or if *he* thinks you're out of his league, then you are. Not because you actually are but because he thinks you are. He's really saying something about himself, not about you. Listen to him.

His Living/Family Room

The Living Room is very important. It's often the first room a guest sees and sometimes the only room. Just like the entry is the first impression, the living room is similar to the first words someone says to you. When looking at the living room, keep in mind that this is his "public" appearance.

As you see the rest of the house, it will be up to you to decide if the living room accurately represents him. If you find the living room is more ready for a relationship than the rest of the house, it is possible he is moving toward being ready and the living room could show that he is a work in progress. It could, however, mean that he presents himself one way but in actuality he is another.

The first thing you want to notice is the available seating. Is it balanced and welcoming for two? Or is it set for one–the lord of the manner–with additional seating that appears to be somewhat of an afterthought?

For example, look to see if his throne is directly in front of the television with maybe another chair off to the side. Also notice if the chairs match or if one is noticeably larger and/or more comfortable than the other. Does "his" chair say "*Ahhh…* I'm going to be sitting here a while" and "her" chair says something like "sit a while but not too long; don't get too comfortable here!"

Also notice if there is a chair/sofa/love seat large enough for two to sit side by side or even lay next to each other. Is his home ready to receive you or will you need to push your way in?

Is the TV large, new and expensive in contrast to the quality of the seating items? He's telling you his priority – entertainment, not stability or comfort. A large TV that dominates the room could dominate his attention. You may have a difficult time prying him away from the television; almost like 'another woman,' unless you want to settle in alongside him. If you do, there is nothing wrong with that. Just be sure that is what you want and not that you are going along with it in order to be near him. Things may never change and one day you may resent being second in line to the TV. Be sure it is a balance that you are not only comfortable with, but *happy* about.

FENG SHUI

Feng Shui (pronounced *fung shway*) translates literally to Wind Water. Figuratively it refers to balance in an environment, being in harmony with one's environment, and the relationship between seen and unseen energy and shapes.

Another thing to consider is if the living room is overrun by kids' toys, pet items, work, or other distractions. If it is, this is probably someone who has a hard time settling in for a relaxing evening without being distracted or interrupted.

The home of a woman I visited had 5 dog beds in the living room, all within a few feet of each other. I learned that the dog had gone through some serious health issues several months previously including a risky surgery. Her dog's health had consumed her life. There hadn't been room in her life for a relationship; there had hardly been room for her work. She wanted her dog to be comfortable while he recuperated so she kept putting beds down: one in the sun, one in the shade, one near the sofa, one near the corner, one near the door…. you get the idea. Her dog's health was now stable so I advised her to put the extra beds away.

Take note of special or temporary circumstances. Sometimes things just become a habit, or blend in after time. People don't think about it after a while. What they do when they are reminded is the key. Like this woman, who immediately removed the extra beds; this showed her willingness to create space for a relationship.

Men are often not only more observant of their surroundings than women are, but they are also more willing to interpret the information they observe and act accordingly. Women tend to ignore, make excuses, or try to "fix" him; men use the information to make decisions and choices. That's not to say they jump to conclusions or find "deal breakers" too quickly. They usually observe, test, and then respond accordingly based on their goals and intentions, choosing what they can and cannot live with or without but not trying to "fix."

Men tend to be more accepting of the way things are and they choose to stay or go based on their intentions and desires. Feng Shui originated in nature where historically men spent most of their time observing and working with their surroundings. Use your "Feng Shui Eyes." Observe his surroundings, interpret and respond accordingly.

Notice what you observe and maybe even comment on it, in a non-judgmental way. And then watch what happens; not only the immediate response but his actions in the short-term. If you choose to stick around for long, see what he does long-term. As long as the room is comfortable for you, there's no issue. However, if there are things that distract you or make you uneasy, pay attention to them.

Notes

His Art

Art is a very personal thing. You may love something that someone else thinks a young, untrained child could have done. We're not talking about "taste" now. Sure taste may come into play in the long run when you are furnishing or decorating a home you share with another person but that is not the primary focus of this book. I'm talking about what his art selection may be able to tell you about his availability for the type of relationship you want.

Look around his home; does he have any art? If so, what kind? What does it look like? How does it make you feel when you look at it? Do you feel warm; welcome; invited/inviting? Or, do you feel like you've just entered a men-only club or, perhaps worse yet, a boy's tree house?

Let's first take a look at blank walls. This could be a great thing: a blank canvas waiting to be enhanced and beautified

14

by a woman's touch. It may indicate an opportunity to create your dreams and goals together, or not… It all depends upon how long he's lived there.

If he's lived there only a short time, it could be a great opportunity to get to know each other by going shopping together for art. You will see where your tastes align and where they differ. If you do find yourself on a shopping spree, depending upon how long you've been seeing each other, you may need to remember that you can make suggestions but the final decisions should be his. You might even find it beneficial to listen to his opinions first.

Let him show you what he likes and is drawn to rather than trying to steer him toward what you like. After all, you are trying to interpret his taste, not convince him of yours! You want to see what he would choose for his walls right now, on his own, so you can gain an understanding of him and of where he is in the relationship spectrum right now.

Ask him questions about the art he picks – what does he like about it? What drew him to it? What inspired him to place it where he did or where he is going to place it? Be careful that you ask in a kind-hearted interested way rather than an interrogating or analyzing way, or you may put him on the defensive and you may not get clear or accurate answers. Instead, he may shut down and you could be teaching him to exclude you.

CLUTTER

There are two types of clutter: Active and Stagnant.

If he's lived there for a while and the walls are still empty that tells you that he is focused on something other than a home. Quite possibly, all that is associated with a home, such as a wife and children, are just not on his radar at the moment. This doesn't mean he is a bad guy, but it is likely an indicator that he is focused on something else right now, not necessarily forever, but for now, so you will have to determine if you are willing to wait and see what happens when/if that changes. Knowing your timeline is a necessity in this instance.

Let me clarify what I mean when I say "he's lived there for a while". It's likely that a person who is ready for a relationship, partnership, spouse, family would have hung at least some art within a year of moving into his residence. Adding art is most likely something that happens over time, gradually adding one or two pieces here or there until the walls have been decorated. If he's lived in his home between one and twelve months, pay attention to how you feel about the number of empty walls based on the length of time he's lived there or has lived on his own.

If he comments about needing a woman's help to pick art listen to that and the reasoning behind it, such as "I have no idea what I want," or "I've been so focused on building my business," or "When I divorced 5 years ago my ex got all the art," or "This art belonged to my mother."

Let me clarify this: Did he mean the paintings or photographs were created by his mother, or is it the art his mother had in her home before she moved to an assisted living home? One may indicate a respect and admiration for his mother's talents the other may indicate that his mother still controls or dominates his life; or that he still needs/allows his mom to guide him.

His reasons for having empty walls will most likely tell you whether he is holding space for a new woman to be in his life; whether he is still holding onto a woman from his past; or if he has unfinished business with his mother or his ex. "My ex took all the art" as an excuse for empty walls may indicate anger, resentment, or bitterness. It may be a fact that his ex got the art, but why keep the empty walls as a constant reminder of that? This may show that he's not emotionally ready for a warm, loving, and balanced relationship. He may stay in it as long as *you* make the effort but he may not be in it as deeply as you would like him to be.

Ok, so what if he has art and it's not from his mother or his ex, what can that tell you about this man? Suppose his walls are filled with framed art; all of it abstract in style. This man may have chaos in his life; nothing is clear. Get it? Abstract? Not clear? He could be setting himself up to have chaos, confusion, and lack of clarity. Suppose most of the art contains one single male figure in the scene; the single male figures in the art send a message about being a lone ranger, or perhaps having intimacy issues. Let's look closer at this.

Let's say the prints are mainly of single men; not one romantic scene around, not one couple or one woman to be found, except in the bedroom. Suppose he has only one scenic piece. Maybe it's a large piece over the sofa. One lone sailboat off in the distance, and in front, "blocking" access, we are looking through jagged, spear-like leaves of a palm tree.

These leaves in the forefront are representative of looking through prison bars. They are also representative of spears cutting at the serenity and peace that is in view beyond the barrier and thus unattainable. Is this an inviting scene or not? It's as simple as that. Sharp, jagged, or pointed-leafed plants, in Feng Shui, represent spears or arrows blocking or guarding access. Or perhaps his one piece of art is the infamous bulldogs playing poker. This may be telling you about the type of activity that generally goes on in this room.

The location of this is important. In the living room this may be a yellow flag to be aware of; in the bedroom it may be more of a concern. If he has a pool table in the "game room," the bull dog picture is perfect. The point being he has a designated space for this purpose and therefore he likely has it in perspective, in balance, in his life.

The examples above came from a client of mine. I tried to explain to him on several occasions how these pictures were keeping chaos and uncertainty alive in his life. I suggested he take the pictures down, all of them, he didn't. Car accident; speeding ticket; car locked in a parking garage overnight; mother had a stroke; and he was interviewed by child services. These things all happened to this man within a two week period!

ACTIVE CLUTTER

Active clutter is the stacks, piles and projects that you are currently working with. Things you are interacting with on a frequent basis. This is a work-in-progress and does not drain energy as long as it remains active.

One couple I worked with had art throughout their home showing women alone, almost looking as if they were waiting for something or someone. When I spoke with the wife, I learned that the husband often worked late or had other business that kept him outside of the home while she sat home, alone, waiting for him. He was in law enforcement so when he was away she was usually sitting, waiting, and worrying. Their art supported this. Although I advised them to remove at least some of that art and replace it with art that had couples in it, they didn't. The last I heard she was still sitting and waiting.

Does he have posters tacked up *á la* college dorm room? Obviously if we are talking about a younger man this may be age appropriate, but for an older man, this is telling you something about his emotional level. Of course, there are exceptions. One example could be that he is in the movie business, and has framed movie posters around.

If there are people in the art, are they "three's a crowd" settings? Does he have supermodels displayed everywhere or sci-fi figures or sports heroes? Ask yourself if it reflects his age and financial status or if it is left-over from long-ago. It may be keeping him in the past behavior pattern and not allowing him to move forward with his achievements.

I'm not saying the rooms need to be filled with priceless art, but does it look age appropriate or does it look like a college dorm? I keep using that reference but let's face it, we've all seen those bachelor pads that we overlook and even get excited about because we interpret it as him being in need of a woman's touch. Ok, let's talk about that.

Sometimes that is true. So offer some suggestions or offer to help redecorate. Is he open to that or does he resist? Although I'm a professional Feng Shui Consultant and clients have told me they've read books on Feng Shui, believe in Feng Shui and have applied Feng Shui, when I've made suggestions about how taking the art off their walls would generate positive changes in their life, some refuse. These people are more attached to the art than committed to the type of relationship they say they want.

STAGNANT CLUTTER

Stagnant clutter is the things that sit idle such as stacks of old magazines or newspapers, projects started months or years ago but have not been worked on since you can't remember when. Stagnant clutter drains energy.

And of course, pay attention to actions over words. If you bring it up, he agrees and yet the pictures don't come down, pay attention to this. Sometimes people want things but not if they have to make changes to get them. They may not be ready to let go of what they have. He may need time to make the transition, so make the suggestion and wait. Give him some time, a few days, a week, a month, and see if he takes action before you turn and run. If it has been a while you may want to bring it up again in a kind way and pay attention to his response. Does it create an opening for communication and growth or does it close a door? Then you'll know if you want to step in or walk away.

The appearance of the non-supportive type of art mentioned earlier, in and of itself isn't the deal breaker. It's possible he, like so many others, purchased things or received them as gifts. There was a bare spot on the wall, he hung it up and then forgot about it. It blends into the wall over time so he doesn't actually "see" it. But it is still there, working on his subconscious mind which leads to the relationships, or lack thereof, in his life.

If your man, or woman, has art that is not in alignment with the type of relationship you want or that he talks about, nudge him to remove it. If he does so, it's likely this is someone willing to create space for new art and a relationship with you. If he resists, that tells you something about him and how he feels about relationships.

Pay attention to whether he tells you directly that he doesn't want to remove the art or whether he agrees with you but then he doesn't follow those words with corresponding actions. These are all indicators of the emotional place he is in. You decide if it aligns with what you are allowing into your life.

I'm not saying that you go into his home on the first date and start redecorating or suggesting to him that he is in need of redecorating. That could send just about anyone packing, and if it didn't, then that should be a warning sign!

You know when it feels like it's time to move the relationship forward and yet it seems to be stuck; that's the time to offer a few suggestions and see how he responds and how the relationship shifts from there. Sometimes a shift in our environment is all that is needed to start to shift things in our relationship and our life.

Just remember, in Feng Shui, it is sometimes better to have a blank canvas, i.e., blank walls that can be used to create any number of things than to have things that are not in alignment with what you say you want. Blank is room to create from nothing without needing to remove or release the old, which is often the difficult part. The excuse of "I can't afford/don't have time to buy new art" should not stop one from clearing out what no longer represents the life he wants to live.

Blank walls are ok for a while and often even favorable, kind of like cleansing the pallet when wine tasting. Just don't leave them blank too long or it could create a new set of issues to deal with.

What's too long? It depends: for some a couple of weeks, for some a few months to a year or more. It all depends upon how clear you are about what you want and how much time and energy you are willing to put into it now to bring it into your life.

LUCK TRINITY

In Chinese Philosophy, how a person's life goes is determined by three types of luck:

1/3 Heaven – Destiny or Timing
1/3 Human – Your Actions
1/3 Earth – Feng Shui

One Feng Shui Master I studied with frequently answered my questions starting with "it depends…" This is so true because there are many factors that impact Feng Shui. Also, Feng Shui is only one factor.

Really look around at what kind of art the apple of your eye has on his walls. Is it art that you like? Is it art that makes you feel good? Is it art that invites romance and a relationship with you? Are there people in it? Are the people doing things you enjoy doing or that you could see yourself doing or that you respect?

If you answered yes to some, most or better yet, all of these questions, then you have a good indicator that this person is looking for and ready for the same things that you want. If you answered no, then take a long hard look at what the art is saying about this person and whether that is compatible with your goals and values.

One man I met had a hobby of reenacting medieval sword fights. His girlfriend thought it was "silly" and almost obsessive. His art and equipment weren't things she respected; therefore living with them would not be favorable *for her*. If she changed that view, so that seeing those things brought her joy because she was reminded of her loving boyfriend, that would be a different story and they would then be favorable. See? It depends…upon her reaction/feelings towards it.

Don't forget to look through your home asking these same questions to make sure that your own environment is in alignment with what you say you want. Notice if your walls are full of solitary women or if they are full of couples. Make changes accordingly to support you in attracting the relationship you desire.

REMOVE 3 THINGS TODAY

Stagnant, sometimes called inactive clutter, drains energy. Active clutter does not. Remove 3 things in your home today that are not supporting a balanced relationship.

Notes

His Furniture

and

Home Accessories

You'll be able to tell a lot from his furniture. I'm not just referring to whether or not it is expensive or you like the style choice; his furniture can tell you so much more. Does the value/cost of his furniture match his current status? Take a look, I mean *really* take a look at his furniture. We all know about the stereotypical Bachelor Pad that needs a woman's touch. But there's a difference between a pad that is open to/waiting for a woman to enter and a pad that says "come visit when I want you to, but don't try to stay." How do you tell the difference? That's easy!

Does the furniture look so worn and dirty that you don't want to sit down? Does he not mind living like this? Do you not mind living like this? It could be hinting at the many past concubines. It's possible you'll be the next before he moves onto yet another. Before you do anything hasty, consider other factors as well.

Does he have books, magazines, newspapers scattered about? If so, look at them. What can you learn about him from them? Does he hunt or fish? Are you an animal rights activist/vegan? Does he follow the financial industry? Do you live in the moment? Maybe he has a trade magazine or pornography. Chances are that if he has soft-porn sitting in plain sight he may be telling you that he's looking for a good time but perhaps nothing serious. Sure many men have pornography in their homes and they usually take the time to put it out of sight when they have a woman coming over. If he doesn't take the time to do this, then essentially his space is already filled with other beautiful women.

He's allowing you to join his harem, but probably not much more than that. Of course there are no hard and fast rules. How does he react when you notice the magazines or videos? Does he apologize? Get embarrassed? Does he quickly gather them up and put them away somewhere? Does he say something arrogant or suggest you watch one of the videos?

His reaction, once you are both aware that they are there, may be even more important to consider than the fact that they were out in plain sight. Are they in plain sight the next time you are invited over? It's possible it was just an oversight or that he's out of practice in having women to his home. You decide if you will cut him some slack this time and see what happens the next time you visit. Again, it's a personal choice.

What else is in plain sight? Are there books around? What type of books? Books are a good reflection of a person's interests and passions. If you see books, whether sitting on the coffee table, or on a bookshelf, notice if there are a variety of subjects. Do you see any books that you have read or have on your bookshelf? And don't forget to notice if the books look like they've been read or if perhaps they are just gathering dust.

People often try, whether consciously or subconsciously, to portray themselves as what they think the other person is looking for. If you appear as the intellectual type, he may portray himself that way to try to appeal to you. If you see no books around but you see a large, flat-screen television, chances are he is more of a couch jockey than a book worm. Don't ignore this point.

There is the possibility that he keeps books in another part of his home, has an active Kindle, or that he watches intellectual or educational television programs. You will need to gather more data before determining this, but don't dismiss the fact that there are no books around and that the television is the focus of this room.

One man's home I was in had the typical black leather sofa and wide-screen television mounted on the wall. However, the television was in proportion to the room rather than dominating the room so it was not the center of attention. His home, although very masculine, was very tasteful. His kitchen, although quite small had been upgraded with granite counters and stainless appliances. His home was a space where most women would feel quite comfortable, a good indicator that this man was welcoming in a relationship.

Look around for photos or memorabilia. I'm not saying to go snooping in drawers and closets and other rooms. I've heard of some women doing that but I'm not recommending it. I am saying notice what is in sight. Photos of friends? Family? Women? Remember it's all about balance.

Having photos of "the guys" is fine. In fact it can be a good thing. These are the people that are important to him, the people who likely have an influence on him, his life, his relationships. What are they doing in the photos? These photos may give you a good indication of how he spends his free time and what (and who) is important to him. If they don't match with what he has said or what you've seen, beware.

Notes

His Kitchen

To many people, the kitchen is the center of the home; the hub; the gathering place. The kitchen can tell you what a person's priorities are or are not. If you get to look in the refrigerator, does he have any real food in it or are there condiments and beverages only?

Think back to the early years of man. What has he "hunted" and brought home to feed you and the village? That's not saying that he needs to be a gourmet cook. Notice if there is anything nourishing to eat; snacks; frozen dinners. Maybe he'd prefer to take you out to dinner every night; either way is fine as long as that's in alignment with your goals.

Does he order pizza every night? Eat frozen food? Does he have plenty of beer but no food? It's not any one thing that is the "magic formula," but ask yourself what you would infer about a person that you've not met just by looking in their refrigerator. If you are a beer and pizza kind of girl and that's what you see in his fridge, great! If you are lobster and champagne and he's beer and pizza, you've got some things to think about. It doesn't mean it can't work out, it just means that you'll both likely have some adjusting to do. If you and he are ok with that, great! If however, either of you aren't willing to compromise, this will be challenging for you both.

---

3 IMPORTANT AREAS

In Feng Shui, traditionally, the three most important areas of a home are the entry, the bedroom, and the stove.

And remember to get the whole picture. Right now my own refrigerator is pretty barren: limited food and several bottles of wine. The wine was left from a gathering I hosted more than two months ago. The wine is there not because wine is a priority for me, but because I drink so little that the bottles are still there.

On the other hand, a woman I consulted with dated someone who had no food in his home except a box of pop tarts and a variety of alcohol. I'm told that the refrigerator, cabinets, wine rack and entertainment center, yes, his entertainment center, were overrun by bottles of various types of alcohol. He reportedly gave her a tour of his alcohol collection that lasted longer than the tour of his home. It raised a red flag about compatibility but she didn't throw in the towel right away.

He invited her to join him and his friends for dinner. She accepted the invitation and that night learned that dinner meant they'd meet at his home around 6pm for drinks and around 9pm they'd head out to eat. Because she didn't drink, this was less than enjoyable for her. He sloughed it off making it sound like it was unusual for the group but when it happened a second time she admitted that they weren't compatible. His refrigerator and kitchen cabinets told her that the first time she'd been to his home and she kept that in mind.

Are there at least two full place settings of dishes? That means 2 *matching* plates, bowls, glasses, mugs, forks, spoons, knives, etc. If he has to piece things together, he's not thinking in terms of partnership or couple-hood; he's thinking of himself and what is necessary to sustain his energy.

For such a person eating is about necessary nourishment to keep moving; it's not likely to be about a dining experience with another person. He is in conquer, sustain, and build mode. He's building his empire. He's not likely to be looking for the Queen for it, not yet anyway. So check your time-table against his; not likely that his will change, so you'll have to be honest about whether you are willing to change yours.

CHI

Chi, or Qi, (pronounced *chee*) is used to refer to Life Energy. There are two types of energy: Sheng Chi which is favorable and Sha Chi which is unfavorable. Often the word Chi is used by itself to refer to the favorable energy.

Perhaps he is happy to take you out every night, but give that some thought to make sure that is what you want. Really think about it. Sure it sounds great. It may even impress your friends that he takes you out to a nice dinner every night, but will it really make you happy? You could miss out on some wonderful opportunities to create something together; to lick each other's fingers; to dance and sing while creating a meal together; to brush up against each other as you walk past one another.

One couple I worked with ate out most of the time. He'd been divorced for four years and continually told her that he wanted to get married again. Every evening was an event that took about 4 hours to get to the restaurant for dinner, eat, and get home. The meal usually got interrupted by one or more phone calls from his mother, sister, son, or ex-wife.

When my client suggested a quiet meal at home, he usually declined the invitation or cancelled. If he insisted on cooking for her, which he did a couple of times, it took four hours as well because he'd get stuck at work; have to stop to shop on the way to pick her up; check in with the various family members; then start cooking; take a couple more phone calls from family...

You get the picture. The action of going out to dinner each and every night was a way, conscious or unconscious, of avoiding intimacy and real connection with another person.

Out at a restaurant there were built-in distract-ions: waiters coming and going; voices overheard from or by the people at the next table; the sound of dishes clanging, etc.

At home there were just the two of them so he seemed to need the distractions of the phone calls to block the possibility of intimacy, real intimacy. He refused to let her help him prepare the meal; again keeping her at a distance and even out of the room he was in! This is another very important point to keep in mind. It's not just what is in the room that matters but it is very important how the room is used and, even more important, *how the room is shared with you when you are there.*

Does he share the room with you comfortably? Does he seem relaxed having you nearby? The gentle touch or kiss as you pass each other indicates a flow of energy between you that is harmonious. He, or you, may want to treat the other by cooking the entire meal yourself and cleaning up afterward. That's fine on occasion. Or better yet, do as much as you can before the other arrives or find a way to include him.

If you are so focused on the meal preparation by yourself it may set the tone for the evening – and isn't the point to connect with the other person and share some time together? I can't stress enough that there are no hard and fast rules. It depends. One dinner done solo doesn't mean he is not willing to connect, but it could be an indicator, so be sure to look at the whole picture.

His Dining Room

Has the dining room been converted to some other use such as a game room, an office, a storage space or exercise area? One home I saw, the owner had converted his dining room into a crash area for his buddies, housing three twin beds for "the guys" to crash on when they'd had too much to drink. If the dining room is converted, is there another place for *two or more* people to sit down to share a meal together?

In Feng Shui, because of the energy in a certain room, we sometimes convert its function. As long as that converted dining room is replaced someplace else in the home, this isn't a concern. Feng Shui doesn't care what purpose the architect intended, it cares about how the energy of a space is used. So as long as there is a room or space to *comfortably* dine in, it doesn't matter that the dining room has been converted.

Is there a television in the dining room or is a television in another room in view of the dining room? The television could act as a third person during your romantic dinner together unless of course you enjoy sitting down to dinner with the television on. Is there a source of music in the room to set the mood for that romantic dinner? Think about the function of the room again. If it's a room meant to use to dine in, there should be space and ambiance to support that unless there is another space for that, for example, a breakfast nook, a breakfast bar, etc.

What condition is the dining set in? One man I worked with had wobbly chairs and a wobbly table to match. We sat down at the table to discuss his space, he got up, bumped the table and I thought it was going to topple over on me. Instead, the class of water he served me spilled on the table and floor. That could have been a champagne disaster in his date's lap. His dining room furniture did not match his claimed income/status level or the image he wanted to portray of himself...or perhaps it did.

When I spoke further with him, he stated that he usually took his dates out to nice restaurants in the early stages and they didn't see his living space until things were already progressing. Dating and romance are very much like sales – each person selling his or her good qualities and hiding or camouflaging his bad qualities. That's natural to not bring up your weaknesses right away, however the timing of letting your true self show may or may not align with the goal of an intimate long-term relationship.

Think of it as playing a trump card or a deal breaker; holding that card you know you can play when the game gets too hot and you want out. It may be done subconsciously, but done nonetheless. So consider not only the style and condition of his furnishings and space, but also the timing of his exposing them to you. Some people don't come right out and end a relationship; they instead say or do things to manipulate the other person into initiating the break up.

Look at patterns. Look for consistency in his home and his words. If his home doesn't align with what he's told you about himself and his life, there is a reason. That is where you then choose if it's in harmony and balance *with* you and *for* you.

Also look at how he shows you his space. Does he invite you over for a nice romantic dinner? Is he watching your reaction, almost anticipating, i.e., hoping, or even daring you to go running? Ladies, trust your instincts. Remember

40

the key is not so much of what he does, says or has, but how those things make you <u>feel</u>; if you don't feel good pay attention to that.

Also remember, Feng Shui is about how a space feels. Yes, how it looks is important, but as a secondary point. In Feng Shui it is said: "safety and comfort first, then add beauty." If it feels good to you, it is most probable that it will also look good to you.

Too often women ignore their feelings and instincts and instead focus on analyzing, changing, or solving the issues. If you find yourself doing this, he's probably not the man for you unless you want to spend your life analyzing, changing, and solving. Some women enjoy that. It may make them feel powerful and in control. For others it's exhausting. Know which type you are and choose accordingly.

TAI CHI

The Tai Chi symbol, commonly referred to as the Yin Yang symbol, represents energy, balance and movement. It demonstrates the interaction between opposites and reminds us, for example, that without dark there is no light, without cold there is no warm.

Let's go back to the idea of the quality/condition of his furnishings not matching the way he has presented himself to you. That should send a loud warning message. What warning? Perhaps it's indicating that he has not been honest about his income/status; perhaps it speaks to his priorities and, more important, what his priorities aren't. If he's not been honest about his status, what else may he have been dishonest about or perhaps withheld from you?

Thinking of the man I've been using as an example, quite honestly, a furnished rental would have had better furnishings than his home. I explained to him that the condition of his living space in contrast to what he had shared with me about him, his life, his work, his income, from a dating perspective, could make a woman question if he perhaps was married and this was his hideaway where he took his unsuspecting prey.

Ladies, when things don't add up, they don't add up. If you ask him about it, do you really think he will say: "Oh, well, I'm actually married, but I cheat on my wife, so I need a place to do that and yet I didn't want to spend a lot of money on it?" Or perhaps he'll say "I'm really broke and unemployed and I knew you wouldn't date me so I told you those things thinking that you'd fall in love with me, or at least sleep with me before you'd find out the truth." Really? Do you think he'll tell you that?

Go ahead and ask him the questions but when the answers aren't clear and straight-forward, and perhaps even if they are, keep your eyes open and your hand on the door knob until you really feel comfortable with all the information you've been given. Trust what you see and be cautious trusting what he says if it doesn't match with what you see.

Here are some additional thoughts and considerations for the table. Is there an even number of chairs around it? Say, perhaps four so you could also dine with another couple? 3 chairs may indicate he's leaving room for a third person.

Are the chairs matching or at least equivalent in size, condition and grandeur? Is there one decent chair that <u>he</u> sits in or does he offer it to you? Are there cushions on the chairs? Are they in good condition or are they lumpy, ripped, or perhaps stained? Are the backs broken or cracked? If so, he may be telling you that he doesn't want anyone to stay long. He may be trying to turn you off so you don't get any ideas about hanging around too long. Or he just may not care about entertaining or impressing anyone, even you. How does that make you feel?

Notes

His Bathroom

The bathroom is another interesting and often misunderstood room. It can be a room of intimacy when shared for the morning grooming rituals or late night shower for two; or it can be a room to lock another out.

Almost every home or apartment has a bathroom door that locks; very few have any other internal doors that lock. Look for signs that welcome a woman such as how clean the toilet is – maybe men don't sit that often, but women sit each and every time. Would you prefer to go to the corner gas station rather than sit on his toilet seat?

Don't get caught in that trap of thinking it's cute and that he needs you to take care of him. In this day and age, many successful, working men would hire someone to clean their home and if he doesn't, either it tells you he isn't as successful as he might want you to think he is, or he may not care about cleanliness, or maybe he doesn't want you to get too comfortable in his man cave. All are things to consider.

Did he make an effort to clean for you? Does he clean better next time? Be honest with yourself, ladies, you know if he is trying to make you feel welcome or if he is showing you that he doesn't care or would prefer that you not get too comfortable. Listen to your inner voice.

Some of the following things may not be considered until further into the relationship, but they are worth mentioning here and are well worth thinking about. Is there room in the drawer/cabinet/closet for some of your things? What if you leave a toothbrush or another item sitting on the counter? Is that ok, or does he tuck it away when you leave and you have to search for it the next time you are there?

Or worse yet, he throws it out. What is his explanation when you ask about it? If he doesn't leave his own things out at all, no big deal, as long as your things are treated the same way his things are treated. I'll repeat that: *as long as your things are treated the same as he treats his things*. That is the point. Are your things treated the same as his or are they treated differently and if so, how so? Are they treated better than his or worse than his? Is he hiding your things? If so, that could be an indication that he's hiding you.

One woman I worked with went to her boyfriend's home and discovered that all of her things had been tucked into a drawer: toothbrush, moisturizer, shampoo, conditioner, etc. When she asked why, he said he had put them away to clean. Although other items, his items, had somehow managed to find their way back to the counter top, hers did not. It was as if he wanted no reminder of her.

Remember, men are visual, so if he is in love with you he enjoys seeing those things that remind him of you. If he had been thinking in terms of being a couple, when his toothbrush came back out, hers would have come out right along with it – a match set, a pair, not to be separated. And who takes a toothbrush out of a holder to clean? Most people move the holder, toothbrush and all.

Upon further inquiry, he admitted to her that he had put her things away because his ex-wife had come over and he didn't want to explain to her about his relationship. What he actually may have been saying was that he wanted to tuck this woman away where he knew she'd be for easy access when <u>he wanted</u> to take her out, but that although he was talking to her about a future, he was not talking about her to others in his life.

What you need to understand is that it's not about the explanation he gives in a situation similar to this; it's about the action itself. He will give any explanation he can because it's possible he doesn't even know why he does some of the things he does. The point being that <u>he does them.</u> The reason is just fluff. Pay attention to actions. A therapist told one woman she needed to cover her ears and open her eyes. This is so true. Pay attention to what you see *and* how it makes you feel regardless of what you hear.

Remember, in Feng Shui, having things displayed in pairs is a tool often used to attract a relationship. So if you are in a relationship with someone who doesn't allow your toothbrush to pair with his, it could be an indication that he's not willing to allow you to pair with him.

PAIRS

Things in pairs can be placed to attract and support a relationship. The pairs should belong together in some way such as being the same size, stature, or color. Do they look like a mismatch or a perfect fit?

Let's say he does treat your things in the same way he treats his things. Then you can also consider how he treats his things. Is it with the same care with which you treat your things? If not, are you ok with that? Best not to deny your feelings, kid yourself, or make excuses. This won't avoid issues, it will only delay them.

Pay attention to how you feel and respond to his environment and how he feels and responds to your environment. After all, Feng Shui is about energy and how you feel and respond to your environment.

Does he come over for short periods of time and then find what seems like any excuse to leave? Does he appear relaxed and comfortable when you are in his space for extended stays, or when he is in yours? Think of someone's space as the first step into their life. Are you welcome or not? Are you both comfortable or not? Make note of this.

Notes

His Bedroom

The bedroom can be one of the most telling rooms. In my consultations I've often described the relationship and the personality of the spouse, whom I've not met, just by looking at the bedroom. So if you are given the opportunity to see his bedroom, be sure to look using your "Feng Shui Eyes." What do I mean by that? Put aside all other thoughts and really look at his bedroom from the perspective of Feng Shui, relationship, romance, etc.

In Feng Shui, the bedroom has two purposes: sleep and romance. Just about anything else is not, I repeat, not welcome in the bedroom. No desk, no television, no book case, no exercise equipment, no trophies; and Ladies, no stuffed animals in your room. Anything that does not work to enhance sleeping or romance has no place in the bedroom.

This includes pictures of friends and family. This is a good indicator that these people will be as much a part of the relationship as you are. In other words, they may occur as interfering, meddling or even coming first more often than is comfortable for you. An additional comment on books: Some books may be okay in the bedroom. The key being the quantity and the types of books he has. Keeping in mind whether it is supportive of sleep and/or intimacy, you will know if the book is better kept elsewhere.

Are both sides of the bed accessible? If so, he wants you to have easy access in and out of the room. He welcomes you and wants you to be comfortable. Or perhaps the bed is pushed up against a wall so that one person would be blocked in (or out) by the other person. This creates a dominant situation; making the relationship off-balance. If you are a very submissive person, wanting to be in the shadow of your man, this could work, otherwise you are likely to be unhappy unless the balance shifts.

This is not an ideal example; see comments on page 59

Are there tables on each side of the bed? Do they belong together? Look at the shape, size, style and condition; if they are identical, great. If not, as long as they look like they are balanced and make a nice pair, its fine.

For example, if one is large and solid and the other is very small and frail, it could indicate the imbalance of his relationships and the imbalance of the relationship you would have with him. Whether the larger, more solid table is on his side of the bed or yours, the relationship will have one dominant person. If he has the larger table he will be dominant; if you have the larger table, you will be put in the dominant role.

If you want to have kind of a parent-child type relationship, one of you being parent and one of you being child, then this will work for you. If that is not what you are looking for, you will likely not be happy and the Feng Shui of this bedroom will not be supportive of what you are seeking.

SLEEPING AND ROMANCE

For good Feng Shui in the bedroom, reserve it for sleeping and romance only. Remove anything and everything that does not enhance sleep or romance, including desks, exercise equipment, televisions, and most bookshelves.

We talked about artwork in Chapter 3 and the pictures and art in the bedroom are particularly important. Are the pictures you see representative of a relationship? Are there pictures of couples and/or romantic scenes? If so, then this is a space that will support and nourish a relationship.

On the other hand, maybe he has the infamous picture of the bulldogs playing poker, or something similar, hanging in his bedroom. Does that inspire romance for you? Chances are when you think of romantic pictures you don't think of poker playing bulldogs, so having this hanging in his bedroom may be telling you something about his lifestyle or his priorities. It could be hinting of what I call the "high school girlfriend." He hangs out with the guys most of the time and when he needs some physical attention from a woman he calls his "girlfriend." She's his only girl, but the guys come first. She's called upon only when he needs her, kind of like that football or baseball glove that sits on the shelf most of the time.

The picture may indicate that the guys are always going to be around and possibly even come first. And remember it's not any one thing that determines if a relationship with this man is going to work for you, it's the overall picture you have after you've put on your Feng Shui eyes and looked around his home.

One man, an artist, had several of his own paintings on the walls of his bedroom. All were of beautiful, large breasted, naked women. Take a minute now and think about how you might feel walking into such a room. Would you feel special, beautiful and unique? Would you feel like one of the crowd? Would you be self-conscious and wonder how you stack up, pun intended, to these women?

If the paintings included handsome, muscular, naked men, that would likely cause a different feeling for you. What if you express your feelings about your reaction to these paintings? Does he argue, dismiss or judge? Does he accuse you of being insecure, or does he validate, understand and make adjustments right then or in the near future?

One woman I worked with had a bit of an understanding of Feng Shui and she told me how the first time she'd spent the night at her man's home, she had a difficult time relaxing for sleep. He had a large mirror on the wall next to the bed and she told him mirrors were challenging for sleeping. He hopped out of bed and took the large, heavy mirror down and carried it into another room. He clearly wanted her to feel comfortable in his home. This is a man open to having a woman in his space and in his life.

Does he have family photos, or perhaps even a shrine to his family, in his bedroom? Then it's possible his family will be in your relationship. Whether he wants it that way or not, the pictures of family and/or friends in the bedroom put the energy of others in the relationship. Do not confuse this with his desire to create or start a family with you or another woman. This is about his family of origin; his involvement with them; and their involvement in his life. Family photos are welcome any place other than the bedroom.

56

SISTERS OF FENG SHUI

Feng Shui and Traditional Chinese Medicine (TCM), which includes Acupuncture, are sister modalities that derive from the Ancient Taoist I-Ching and utilize the 5 Elements of nature for balancing: Wood, Fire, Earth, Metal and Water.

I worked with a man who lived out of state who sent me photos of his home. There was no real furniture in the home. Not even a bed. Just metal shelving units! When I asked him about this, he explained that he wanted to be in a relationship, but since any woman he met would likely have a bed, he didn't think he needed one.

I tried to explain to him that a woman who had a bed (and other furniture) would likely be looking for a man who had the same. She would not be interested in a man who had only metal shelves for furniture. He didn't understand the point I was trying to make. He didn't understand that the energy balance was off. He needed to match his vibration to the vibration of the type of woman he wanted in his life.

The fact that he didn't understand this is even more important than his lack of furniture. His resistance to what I was saying spoke loudly of his resistance to be in a *balanced* relationship. His seemingly logical thinking alluded to the possibility that he was looking for a female to rescue him, or perhaps a mother figure; but definitely not an equal partner.

Another man, quite wealthy and from a wealthy family, was divorced, had a son, and lived in a one-bedroom apartment. There were two beds in the one bedroom; one for him and one for his son. Pause. Yes, a bed for him and a bed for his son in the same room. Even the best possible scenario here would involve an empty bed for a child in the room even if the child wasn't there.

There was also a shrine to his son in the room. There must have been ten or twelve framed 8 ½ x 11 photos of his son in the room. There was no way that this could be considered romantic or supportive of a relationship, Feng Shui or otherwise. As much as this man wanted to have female companionship, his son came first. There really wasn't room for anything more than an interlude here and there, until he relocated to an appropriate living space for a man with a child.

BEDROOM

It is best to place art with calm, quiet, peaceful scenes in the bedroom to support rest. Active or high-energy scenes such as animals running or athletes can bring energy to the room and cause sleep to be less restful.

Granted, these are extreme cases but I think the point is clear: The bedroom is for sleeping and romance, not family, or work, or exercise or anything else. Sleeping and Romance. The room should be set up to support this, with a bed, two bedside tables, romantic pictures, etc. Sleeping and Romance. Lounge chairs, loveseats, and restful furniture are all fine. Remember this. If anything else is represented in the room, be wary. The exception to this is, well, none.

Look at the example of a college dorm room, it has several functions. Is a College student's focus on romance and a balanced relationship? Not likely. Their focus is likely on school, being away from home, parties, girls/boys, and hooking up.   It's time to outgrow the multi-purpose bedrooms of our childhood that were used for sleeping, studying, entertaining our friends, and escaping our parents and siblings. Adults are well-advised to reserve their bedroom for sleeping and romance only.

Before moving out of the bedroom it's necessary to address mirrors. Mirrors in a bedroom can cause sleep challenges because mirrors activate energy. It's best to remove them or at least cover him when you are sleeping. You can cover them with a blanket, towel, sheet or a lovely piece of fabric.

If you have mirrored wardrobe doors consider hanging a curtain rod and curtains to cover them. This way, you can put the curtains to the side during the day to give easy access to the closet and the mirrors. At night you can draw the curtains giving the illusion of a window that is quieted for the night.   The softness and flow of the curtains give some femininity to the room and femininity breeds romance. Mirrors don't aid sleep. If however the mirrors are used to aid romance, they can stay, but consider covering them for sleep.

COMMENTS ON PHOTO PAGE 52

Overall this room has a nice balanced feel. The bed has easy access on both sides. The matching side tables are a good foundation of balance, along with the matching lamps on each table. However, mirrors are not ideal in a bedroom, nor are groupings of three conducive to a balanced partnership. The spikey plant on the right is not warm and inviting; it off-sets the chair but is not necessarily balanced. Two plants, with rounded leaves on the right and a bench for two on the left may be a more harmonious arrangement.

Notes

His Closet

(and Yours)

The closet; listen up, Ladies. Women are usually guiltier of bad Feng Shui in the closet than men. To make sure you really hear this, I'm going to direct this first part to you; and you may find that you have work to do in your own closet. Is there room in your closet for a few of his things? A full closet can mean that there is a certain point up to which you will let him into your home and your life but after that, there is a block. As mentioned previously, this holds true for dresser drawers, too.

There is something intimate about your clothes hanging next to each other's in the closet; or going to the closet together to get your clothes for the day; or removing your clothes together in the evening. Are you willing to miss out on these luscious moments of intimacy by banishing him to the hall closet or guest room closet? This one point almost always gets argument from the audience when I give a lecture. When you are a closet hog you are essentially saying that it is more important to you to have all of your clothes near you than it is for you to have your man near you. Think about that. Clothes near; man far.

This doesn't mean that the first time you spend the night together that closet and drawer space need to be provided. When things have progressed to where you are spending the night frequently and consistently, does he make room for you to have some clothes there? Or do you have to pack an overnight bag each time or head home early in the morning to shower before going to work?

Does he create the space for you and/or verbally offer to make room for some of your things? Or do you have to bring up the subject? If you do bring up the subject, how does he respond? Look carefully at his verbal response and at his actions or lack thereof.

One man I spoke with had a history of quick, intense relationships. As he showed me through his home, he pointed out that he had two roommates, one of which was his former live-in girlfriend. She now had a separate room in his home rather than sharing his room. I made note of that.

As we continued our tour, I learned that her clothes were still occupying the closet and dresser drawers in the master bedroom, his room. And she occasionally helped herself to the use of the bathtub in the attached master bathroom.

He insisted this wasn't a problem for them because there was no longer any romantic interest between them. He proudly "proved" his point by adding that she had a boyfriend. He resisted what I had to say on this subject. He argued that this did not interfere with his relationships. He denied that it kept a piece of himself unavailable to other women. He insisted that the cord between them had been cut. And yet, he stated that his roommate's boyfriend didn't like her living there with him and wanted her to move out. No surprise there!

LET YOUR CLOSET... BREATHE

Every breath has an inhale and an exhale. This concept exists in Feng Shui, too. Inhaling is the bringing of things into your space, exhaling is the clearing of things out of your space. To keep balance, it's helpful to practice exhaling along with the inhale.

If you are a clothes hound, or a pack-rat, you may want to try this practice: for each new item you bring into your closet, remove one older item. This will keep balance – inhale and <u>exhale</u> or release. Pick something that no longer expresses who you are or who you want to be and release it.

Shortly after my visit he advised his roommate to remove her things from his room. When she hadn't done so in a timely manner, he purchased storage units and moved her things out to the garage. This is a great indicator that this man, if not ready now, wants to be ready for a balanced relationship in his life and is willing to take action to have one.

Something else to consider if he is spending at least as many nights at your home as you are at his: does he leave things at your home; does he leave early in the morning; or late at night? Or perhaps he packs a gym bag each time and declines your offer to leave some of his things at your home. Men "mark" their territory. If he's not doing that, he's not yet ready to claim you; not even if only to fend off his competition.

Ladies, a note to you on the concept of breathing: Keeping your skinny clothes may actually discourage you in your weight loss goals. They often don't inspire but serve to make us feel bad about the weight we've gained. Besides, most women will want to celebrate reaching their weight-loss goal by buying new clothes! By removing your skinny clothes from your home, you will be practicing breathing and will remove negative reminders from your closet.

Pay attention to how you <u>feel</u> when you spend the night at his place or he spends the night at yours. Also pay attention to how you feel about whether you are doing the inviting or he is. Be aware of how you feel about the balance.

One woman I met with had a boyfriend that lived about 30 miles away. In the years they'd been together, he came to her home only once or twice a year, but she went to his home nearly every weekend. In talking further with her, I learned that to her not being alone was worth driving the 60 miles round-trip each weekend. It wasn't surprising to me when I learned there was a lot of conflict between them.

For many women, always going to him would breed resentment over time; because it goes against our nature: Yin is inward, Yang is outward. In the above case he was staying in and she was going out to him. Most women feel it when the balance is off. How that balance looks will be different for each woman and each relationship. Feng Shui is not "cookie cutter," it is unique for each individual, home, and year.

Notice that the closet is a metaphor. His closet and his willingness to share it with you has an impact on the ease with which you can comfortably stay in his home, which in turn is likely to be an indicator of his willingness to let you into his life. There's the possibility that he is assuming that you know you are welcome to leave some of your things there. If you think this is the case, test it. Leave a few of your things there and see how he reacts. Does he remind you that you left them there? Does he offer them to you? Or are they silently welcomed.

Also notice if the decision of being together and at whose home is a shared one, or if it always his. Is it joint or shared in some way or does he always determine whether you are together and where you are together? Do you invite him to stay with you or does he ask if you would like him to stay? Does he announce that he is leaving or just get up and leave? Do you feel compelled to let him stay if he asks to stay with you?

Remember he may lead by doing the inviting, but you always have the option of declining or offering an alternative suggestion. It's good to do this sometimes; it creates a bit of a blip on the radar instead of it just flat-lining all the time. You might find that he appreciates you more if you aren't always readily available to him.

EVERYTHING IS CONSTANTLY CHANGING

One tenet of Feng Shui is that everything is constantly changing. Check in with yourself to make sure that your feelings have not changed; or that circumstances have not changed in a way that things are no longer in alignment with what you want in your life.

A little yang inside the yin keeps the balance and harmony. Just as the Tai Chi symbol contains yin and yang. It's the opposite energies together that make it what it is. Night isn't night if there is no day to contrast it. So remember that you have choice in every situation. If you find yourself fitting into his schedule, try not doing that and see if he then makes more of an effort to fit into your schedule or if you just don't see each other as often. You may not like the results but you will get invaluable information from this exercise.

Notes

His Car

Is his car date ready? Is it a car that you would be proud to step into or out of on a date? Is the passenger seat clear of items? Or is it a storage space that needs to be cleared off each time you get in? If the seat is usually full of stuff then it may be a signal to you that this person doesn't have room for you. He seems to be making a production out of making room for you. And worse yet, he is doing it in front of you while you stand around waiting. This could be symbolic of the relationship. Perhaps you will be waiting for him to meet your needs and for him to decide if you fit into his lifestyle.

With the popularity of telecommuting, it's not uncommon for people to keep a lot of things in their car. Many men get their car washed before a date. *Before* being the keyword here. If he picked you up for dinner in a dirty car and then stopped at the car wash on the way to the restaurant most of us would question the appropriateness of that. Why then would you overlook the seat clearing or him stopping at the cash machine after picking you up? This could indicate that he wants credit for his effort and thus he makes a show out of clearing the seat for you or some other similar action. It may be an indicator of him seeing it as too much effort rather than him being a provider of joy. Would you ask him to wait while you get a mani/pedi? Not likely.

The point being is he ready for the date when he arrives or not? Ready. Not almost ready, not asking you to wait while he gets ready. Do you see the symbolism here? Ready for the date is a good indicator that he's ready for the relationship.

And what about the type of vehicle he drives? Let's say he has a truck; that may be fine if you are a sporty/athletic person, but if you like fine dining and the theatre, chances are you won't be comfortable getting dressed up and then having to struggle to climb in and out of his truck. An SUV may be a similar scenario – that is indicative of hauling things, children, or buddies around. It can be telling you what his life is all about so give that some consideration. Remember, I'm not just talking about whether his car is expensive or not, it's about taste and style. If expensive is your taste and style, then by all means give that consideration, too.

Notice what he keeps stored in his car. Does he have old fast food wrappers? A change of clothes? Athletic gear? These will all be indicators of his lifestyle and how he spends his time. Does he have clutter in his trunk? Remember the difference between active and stagnant clutter. If his trunk is full of things that he never uses, why does he haul them around with him everywhere he goes?

Clutter in the trunk could be an indicator of "baggage" in his subconscious. Is it in the back seat? Maybe he sees his issues but is choosing not to deal with them.

Does he keep first aid or emergency items in his vehicle? Water bottles? Jumper cables? Tools including a jack? Take into account the climate and road conditions where you live and that will help you properly evaluate the items he does or does not keep in his vehicle. For example, a blanket in the South may be a nice to have item for an impromptu picnic, but in the North, a blanket may be a necessity in the winter months.

All these are indicators of his personality type. For example, you will discover if he is a risk taker or if he plans ahead. This will likely align with his dating style. Does he call you last minute or call you during the week to make plans for the weekend? There is no right or wrong here, just a matter of style preference. You must first be honest with yourself about your style preference to be able to evaluate if he is a good match for you long-term.

Does he have a cell phone charger? His laptop? These too are good indicators of his personality type. Is he prepared to handle issues that come up? This could mean having a AAA card or jumper cable and jack. Either way, he has a plan in the event of a roadside issue. Phone charger and laptop? He could be ensuring that communication lines are open and accessible and it's likely he will approach his relationships the same way. It could also indicate that he is always working, and you will figure this out soon enough.

His driving style will also tell you something about his personality. We all have bad days on the road. For some that may mean being preoccupied and missing their turn, for others it may mean rushing around late for appointments. Look at the pattern. Is he courteous to other drivers? Does he use turn signals? I view turn signals as a form of communication: communicating with other drivers. Someone who habitually neglects to use them may be so focused on themselves that they are dismissive of those around them: on the road and in their life.

How does he treat pedestrians or other drivers wanting to change lanes or merge into traffic? Is he a risk taker when he changes lanes or merges? These are all things to observe and consider. In other words is his driving style similar to Mario Andretti or the Little Old Lady from Pasadena? His driving personality is likely a reflection of *his* personality so make sure that it aligns with you, your personality, and what you are inviting into your life. If he's an Andretti and you're a Pasadena, or vice versa, you'll likely be uncomfortable whenever you are a passenger in his car.

That will in turn likely lead to discomfort, frustration, and arguments in and out of the car.

One final thought on the subject of movement; also observe his style of walking. Does he jaywalk, cutting across busy roads, pausing (or not) in the center of the busy road waiting for oncoming traffic to pass? Does he expect you to do the same? If this is your own style, no problem. However, if you are the kind of person that will walk down the road to the cross walk rather than take the risk of dodging traffic beware if he expects you to follow him through the obstacle course of crossing in the middle of the road.

You could find yourself feeling anxious, frustrated, insecure, or unsafe with him; in his car, walking down the street, and in the relationship. You may find it intriguing to visit that style, for a while. It may feel exciting and exhilarating at first, but over the long-term it could create conflict and discomfort for you. The reverse is also true. If you are the risk taker and he plays it safe, you may find yourself feeling bored and dragged down in this relationship. Know your style and observe his, then you can make wise choices for yourself and your relationships.

His Place of Work

What does his place of work have to do with your relationship? He is likely to spend more of his waking time there than with you, and it's sure to have an impact on your relationship. Depending upon the type of work he does, you may or may not be able to check out his space. Also dependent upon the type of work he does, he will have more or less control over his work environment.

If he has some space to call his own (an office, a cubicle, a desk, a station, or even a counter) does he add his personal things to the space and if so, what kind? Does he have photos of you? Family? Friends? Pets? Does he have games and toys? Does he have musician or movie posters/pictures?

Do the personal items reflect his age and way of life? Does he reflect a man of his age ready for a relationship? And do they reflect *your* age, way of life, and what you arelooking for? Do they change over time growing with your relationship?

Seeing his work space may give you insight to the man he is when you aren't around. It's possible he may make some adjustments to his space if he knows in advance you are coming to visit, but over time this will be brought to light so don't put a lot of energy into playing detective about this. Those things will make their way back out and he won't remember or have time to put them away next time. Or better yet, one day they *won't* make their way back out which will indicate he's that much closer to being ready for what you are seeking.

Is his office neat or cluttered? Is it the same as his home or the opposite? A neat home and cluttered office may indicate issues with power, success, or authority because clutter often shows up in the areas where we have resistance.

Also pay attention to how he speaks of his work and his co-workers. Does he talk about it as if he's part of a team working toward a goal? Does he talk about it as if it's temporary and if so, does he talk of his next intended step? Does he talk about it with pride or with embarrassment? One woman told me about how important her boyfriend's work was and yet the one time he allowed her to come to his office he didn't introduce her to anyone there, note even the person in the office next to his. She simply smiled politely, and awkwardly, as they passed his co-workers. Do you see that he wasn't fully letting her into his work space?

Additionally, this man's office looked sterile. Over time she learned that was how he was – no real connection or intimacy. Remember there is a difference between being in need of a woman's touch and being shut down. One is masculine or yang energy that is asking to be balanced with feminine or yin energy. The other is more like a young boy's tree house that says "no girls allowed," perhaps indicating he is closed or guarded; maybe recovering from a break up and not ready to reconnect with a woman.

Look for signs of alignment in his words and his actions. In the example above the man's words "work is important" didn't align with his actions of not introducing her. Or perhaps they did…it's possible his work was important but he may not have held her in that same high regard. Look for alignment and how or *if* he brings you into his work world and *how you feel*.

There are some other things to consider regarding how he speaks of his work. His words will indicate whether he wants to be there or not. If he's unhappy, why is he

78

staying? Is it in order to pay a large home mortgage? This may indicate something about his need for a certain public image regardless of his own personal happiness. Maybe he's trying to please someone else. Men (and women) usually treat their significant others in the same manner they treat themselves. So if he puts others before himself, he will likely put others before you also. Are you ok with that? If the large mortgage is something for which you too will tolerate an unsatisfying job then he could be a good match for you. It all goes back to goals and the effort he, and you, are willing to put forth to reach those goals.

Some women like to nurture their man. So if he is unhappy in his job and you like to be a sounding board or offer solutions, or even just commiserate with him, you could be happy together. Be sure that he is willing to hear your ideas and suggestions, though. If you are action oriented and take steps to change things rather than being accepting of things as they are, you are not likely to be happy long-term with someone who stays in a job that is dissatisfying.

Pay close attention to your work styles. If you are constantly striving for advancement and he's not, this partnership could have a rocky road ahead. If he on the other hand is constantly striving for advancement and the ability to have the best money can buy, he will likely be away from home, and you, often. That could change over time if he has set goals he is trying to attain, but if he is the type to always be going for the next golden ring, will you be happy if he is away from you that often?

If his job doesn't satisfy him he may have a difficult time being in a healthy balanced relationship unless he is accepting of the choices he has made and continues to make by staying at the job. That doesn't mean he must love every aspect of his job but, keeping with the same example of the large mortgage, if he loves the house with the large mortgage and he chooses the job to be able to keep that house, then does he appreciate the job for what it provides or does he complain about it? Does he show his appreciation by having successes at work or does he just slide by?

Remember, men are natural providers and protectors so if he is dissatisfied with his job, i.e., his ability to provide, he may not be ready for the type of relationship you are seeking.

All of these things could reflect his way of life and his current mind-set. Pay attention, observe, be aware and *always trust your feelings*.

His Pets

Most pet owners love their pets. It's getting more and more common to consider pets as part of the family rather than an object or a possession. Pets often share our home rather than being confined to the outdoors. Some pets even have their own rooms.

Although the type of pet he has is important from the standpoint of compatibility with your preferred pet type, here I invite you to focus on the amount of pets and how they move around the home, rather than the type.

Pets sleeping on the bed; there is no hard and fast rule on this as long as there is still room for you in the bed and you don't mind the pet in the bed. Remember the *pet should fit in around you not the other way around* – you shouldn't have to fit in around the pet.

Ladies, take heed of this advice yourself. I see no Feng Shui issues with pets sleeping on our beds as long as they know they are guests there. In other words, when there is another person sharing your bed, you and the pet give him the alpha position over the pet. Both your man and your pet should know their hierarchy.

One man had a number of pets. As I recall he had 2 dogs, 3 cats, 3 rabbits, 2 guinea pigs and 2 birds. If he lived on a farm with lots of open space, no problem but he lived in Los Angeles and all of these animals were in his home, mainly in his living room. They came out of their cages in shifts, each species getting its time to run free.

It seemed to me that he had a lot of pets around for two reasons: 1) it kept a barrier between him and other people and 2) he could control the animals a lot easier than he could control people. He took the animals out when it was convenient and desirable for him. Otherwise they were tucked away like a baseball glove, a sweater, or a DVD. He also had a job that required him to work evenings, weekends and holidays; again, a potential barrier between him, others, and a relationship.

MAHATMA GANDHI

"The greatness of a nation and its moral progress can be judged by the way its animals are treated."

Another man I spoke with had 5 dogs. All the animals were rescues that he happened upon or rather, from the sounds of it, they happened upon him. These rescues all crossed his path and he was unable to resist them. Was he a bleeding heart or a good-deed-doer? I learned that he was struggling to find work and was at risk of losing his home because he had been having difficulty paying his mortgage.

Taking on pets, like choosing to have children, should be considered carefully based on the time you have to dedicate to them; your daily routine and travel schedule, and of course your financial ability to care for them properly without causing an unnecessary burden. Perhaps when he acquired the animals, he was in a more stable financial situation. If so, it could be a good sign that he didn't abandon them when hard times arrived. However, pets, and children, can be used as barriers placed between their owners and the possibility of an intimate relationship, especially 5 pets.

Looking at pets from another direction, pets can move energy through a home so depending upon where they sleep, eat, or eliminate, various energies will be spread through the home, activated or drained. Look at who runs the home. The dog may have free movement in the home for example and still know its place. In other cases, the dog runs the home. Not only is this not good Feng Shui, it is also an indicator of the personality of the owner.

Think carefully about getting into a relationship with someone who has a pet that you don't like or it doesn't like you. I know of cases where the long-time pet was given away when the relationship progressed to cohabitation and one partner didn't care for the other's pet.

Are you willing to give up your pet for another person? Would you expect someone else to give up his pet for you? Would you be willing to get allergy shots? Would you be willing to "quarantine" your pet to one room or an area in the home if your boyfriend didn't like the pet or was allergic? And what if he is willing to give away his pet for you? Would you feel honored by that or would you be worried about the ease with which he cast off a beloved pet and then wonder how easily he would be willing to trade you in for another?

There is no right or wrong. Remember Feng Shui is about how you feel; how an energy impacts you or how you respond to that energy. Be honest, how would you feel about him giving away a pet? Maybe it would depend upon factors such as the type of pet or how long he'd had the pet. Think about it carefully.

Of course there is the view that his animal may seem more important to him than a relationship. There is no right or wrong, just know how you feel and pay attention to that. If you feel second to the animal, that will drain you of vital Chi, Life Energy. If he gives up his animal for you, will you feel guilty, wonder what happened to that animal, or wonder when he will send you away?

Notes

His Activities

What do his activities have to do with Feng Shui? Feng Shui is the study of the impacts on us of space and time. Space and *time*.

Although the time part of Feng Shui is traditionally referring to how something changes over time or is impacted by the time it was built, occupied, or renovated, it is worth looking at how this man spends his time.

Does he budget his time? Does he squander his time? Does he fill his time so there is no room for you? Take a look at how he fills his schedule. Feng Shui is about balance. Is his schedule such that he has balance in his life? Does he have a balance of activities or is there an imbalance? Perhaps he's a workaholic or a sports fanatic. Remember, it's about balance. If it's playoff time and he's watching more sports than usual, cut him some slack.

If he's working on a big project or working towards a promotion so he's spending long days at the office, cut him some slack. If he continues to spend an excess of time watching sports after the playoffs, think about how that will impact your life if the relationship continues. If the promotion doesn't come or there's another project after this one, or maybe he gets the promotion and now has to work long days because he's in a new position, think about that. Will there be another project, or promotion, after this one, and another, and another?

SPACE AND TIME FENG SHUI

One of the oldest styles of Feng Shui is often referred to as Flying Star because of the movement of energy within a structure. Its traditional name is Xuan Kong.

What if he is a ski bum and you are a sun bunny? This could present challenges in selecting vacation spots unless you are both willing to do what the other enjoys even if it is not your idea of the ideal vacation. If he skis, snowboards, hunts, fishes or any other seasonal activity then you will need to consider how often he does these things and whether or not you are willing to join in and/or be apart frequently. It's all about knowing your needs. That is of critical importance.

If you are a woman who doesn't want to spend much time away from her man, then you will be wise to choose someone with similar activities. If you like having time apart to do your own thing, be sure you are clear on how much time and how often. If he golfs and you don't, an afternoon apart each week may be ideal for you, but if he goes on weekend ski trips and leaves you home, know if you will be ok with that or not.

These are all things to consider. Some may be more important later in the relationship than at the earlier stages. Also think about what is most important to you. If you want a life with the best money can buy, it may require him to continue to work those long hours well into the future, so you will need to think about whether the things are more important to you than time spent with him.

Balance is different for each person, so know your needs and you will be better equipped to find your personal balance. And don't forget to make room in *your* schedule for him. Prepare your space and your time for the relationship you are looking for.

The Date

We've all heard statements like: "There are 8 single women for every single man" or "As a woman reaches the age of 40 the chances of marrying decrease more and more." This has led to some women becoming increasingly masculine in their approach to dating. They pursue, they make the adjustments to their schedule to see him; and they go to him.

These things tend to get women sex and surface relationships, but most men who are genuinely interested in a woman want to take care of her. He will go to her so that she is comfortable in her own space rather than asking her to come to him, especially at night. Face it ladies. That is just a bootie call!

Careful, though, watch for the extreme in the other direction. If he seems resistant to you spending the night at his house, that is a way of excluding you.

This masculinization of women in dating can create issues; it throws off the balance. Feng Shui is based on balance. Yin and Yang: Yin feminine; Yang masculine. If you become more yang, you'll likely attract yin men and/or you'll create friction with your yang man. Think about this: men naturally compete.

If you behave more masculine, you set yourself up to compete with your man. Or you may find the yang men disappearing and the yin men coming around. So unless you want to be the "man" in the relationship, you would be wise to resist your urge to "hunt" when you are feeling a scarcity of men. Instead, practice being yin. Be quiet, and let the yang energy come to you almost like a magnet.

That doesn't mean sitting in your home waiting for Prince Charming to knock on your door. It means putting yourself out at places where suitable men are, smiling at them, and *letting* them approach you.

POWER POSITION

The power position is just that, the position of power, authority, or strength. It is protected from behind by a mountain or mountain-like feature such as a wall. To the front is the water: the activity or access point. Traditionally this was used for strategic army placement limiting the possibility of being attacked from behind and ensuring that the enemy would approach from the front and thus not be taken by surprise. It is sometimes referred to as the belly of the dragon or "armchair" position.

Before the relationship, there must be a date. Often that means coffee or sharing a meal. In this situation, be sure that you let him sit in the "power position" with his back protected and a view of the door or activity.

Men are natural providers and protectors. It's in their genes. He will be more relaxed and able to focus on you and your conversation if he is seated in the power position. After all, you want him to hear what you are saying and this is a simple way to ensure that.

If you sit in the position of power, he'll be distracted by any noise or activity occurring behind him. He won't be able to focus on you, what you are saying, or even what he is saying. Remember he is a protector. When a normal, healthy male is around a female, he feels it is his responsibility to protect her. If he is vulnerable, he won't be able to protect himself or her. So, if you need to be in control and you take the power position, know that you will be sacrificing his attention in order to have control.

Thus Power position   addresses his natural protector instinct. Let's look at the other part of this, the provider instinct.   When the bill comes, does he pay it unobtrusively? Or does he comment about it by saying it was a lot of money or perhaps saying what a bargain the meal was?

Either way, he's bringing attention to the act of providing. This may indicate that he is a weak provider or perhaps he is seeking acknowledgment. If you appropriately expressed appreciation for the meal, this may be an indicator that he needs a lot of acknowledgment so you will need to consider if you are willing to give that or not.

Expressing acknowledgment and appreciation comes easy and naturally for some; they enjoy doing it. For others, it may feel awkward, uncomfortable or even fake. So this is another subjective point, and it will depend upon your preferences. Know yourself and you'll be better able to achieve a harmonious date that is more likely to lead to a harmonious relationship.

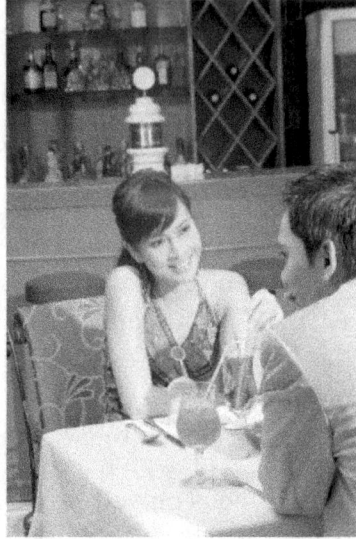

Remember there are many ways to provide, not just financially. So know what you are looking for and observe what he is offering. If you are not seeking financial support from your partner, know what you are seeking. Observe what he is providing; maybe it is time, attention, knowledge, connections, stimulating conversations, compliments, or any number of other things. Be sure what he is offering is what you are seeking. Be honest with yourself and you will make wiser choices.

Notes

Now What?

Now that you've reviewed his space, his time, and his Feng Shui, what do you do with the information you've gathered? Well that is up to you. It isn't a formula that if he "failed" a certain number of these observational points then you should stop seeing him; it's more about seeing how many of these situations pertain to your guy and his environment and also knowing where you are. How many are you comfortable with?

If he has good Feng Shui on most points but not so good on a couple, there is a good chance that a balanced relationship with this person is entirely possible.

If most observations were eye-opening and only one or two were hopeful, you may be in for a difficult road ahead if you want a balanced, committed relationship with this person. There are no hard and fast rules. Know what your limits are and you'll be a Master of the selection process. Below are important factors to consider, listed in order of importance:

How You Feel

First and foremost pay attention to how you feel. This will always be your most important indicator of whether this relationship will make you happy. All relationships have ups and downs so don't make a simple argument mean this won't work for you, but do pay attention to the balance of the good feelings you have about him/the relationship versus the worries, questions, and hurt feelings.

What You See

What you see is also important and definitely worth noting. And pay attention to how you <u>feel</u> about what you see.

What He Does

What he does will speak volumes about how he thinks and feels, and what you can and cannot count on from him.

What He Says

Finally, listen to what he says. Does it align with what he does? If not, what he does is a far more important statement to hear than what he says.

ARE YOU AN EXPERT OR A MASTER

An Expert knows the Rules.
A Master knows the Exceptions.

Consider yourself a Master, and now that you've thoroughly observed your guy's environment, how do you feel about the results of your Feng Shui survey of his home? What are your rules and what are your exceptions?

If you feel good, congratulations! If you don't feel so good, then perhaps it's a good thing you know what you now know before you put more time, effort or energy into this relationship. Perhaps you will choose to free yourself up to let another man flow into your life with whom you will have a better balance, a more harmonious energy, better Chi. If you are still not sure, use the Guide on the following pages.

Quick House Guide

Place an X in each box to indicate this area of his home is Feng Shui ready for a relationship. Do the same for your home.

Are both of you ready for the same thing?	HE	SHE
Foyer/entry is open and inviting		
Living/family room is fit for a King *and* Queen		
Art supports a couple in a balanced relationship		
Clutter is kept to a minimum and is not stagnant		
There's room for two Chefs		
The dining room is the perfect setting for a romantic dinner for two		
The bathroom is guest friendly		
The bedroom is a romantic getaway for two; there's room for no more or no less		
Care to join me in the closet?		
Your chariot is ready and awaits *you*		
Work isn't my life, it supports my life		
Pets know their place, and so does their owner		
Activities are in balance		
What a great date!		
TOTAL- Count the number of Xs in his column and in yours and then read the following page		

Scoring

0-7: Work is needed to prepare his space for a balanced relationship. It could be a long road.

8-11: Almost there! Just some fine-tuning needed. You may want to stick around while this man does his fine-tuning.

12-14: Wow! He's a catch! He is ready, willing and able to allow in a balanced relationship. Are you???

More important than the actual score, is that the two of you scored similarly. If the scores are within a few points of each other, then this could be the relationship you need right now and it could grow into the perfect relationship for you if you both continue to work on preparing your space, and yourselves, for the perfect relationship.

If you scored more than a few points higher than he did, there are likely to be challenges and you will feel frustrated and discontent. You can try to help him shift into range but be careful that you don't create a co-dependent situation where you are trying to "fix" or "change" him, mother him or nag him. Ask for what you want, wait, and see how he responds.

If he scored more than a few points higher than you did, be careful. This man is ready and men go after what they want so if he is in search of a relationship and you aren't ready, or don't get there quickly, he will likely find someone who is. Men tend not to try to fix or change, they just keep looking for what they want until they find it.

The Beginning

The beginning

Coming Soon!

Are You a Princess...
Or a Pauper?

What Your Home's Feng Shui Reveals About You

The second in the

Walls *Do* Talk

Series

By

Helen Arabanos

Recommended Reading

The Western Guide to Feng Shui for Romance
Terah Kathryn Collins

The Yin & Yang of Love, Feng Shui for Relationships
Shan-Tung Hsu, Ph.D.

The Complete Idiot's Guide to Feng Shui
Elizabeth Moran, Master Joseph Yu,
and Master Val Biktashev

Move Your Stuff, Change Your Life
Karen Rauch Carter

Clear Your Clutter with FENG SHUI
Karen Kingston

Who Moved My Cheese
Spencer Johnson, M.D.

The Four Agreements
Don Miguel Ruiz

The Alchemist
Paulo Coelho

The Knight in Rusty Armor
Robert Fisher

Keys to the Kingdom
Alison A. Armstrong

The Proper Care & Feeding of Husbands
Dr. Laura Schlessinger

About the Author

Helen Arabanos was born and raised in Minneapolis. She graduated from the University of Minnesota with a B.A. in Statistics. She started her career in the field of Market Research Analysis and moved into the field of Technology, with an emphasis in Call Center Management and data analysis.

How does somebody with a background in statistics and technology become a Feng Shui Expert? Helen became fascinated when she realized how practical Feng Shui is. Surprisingly, many of the same skills are used. Skills that make her such a qualified Feng Shui Practitioner: data gathering, data analyzing, and making recommendations based on the analysis of data.

In the mid 1980's Helen was introduced to Feng Shui by a man from China at a chance lunch-time encounter. From there she began her quest for more information on this ancient subject. Yet, she remembers that when she was a child, maybe 8 years old, she use to draw floor plans, cut out furniture shapes and place them around the floor plan based on how she felt. She placed them at angles and felt that certain colors were needed in each area. At the time she wasn't aware that she was tuning into the energy and what was needed to create balance.

Helen is a graduate of the Western School of Feng Shui in San Diego, California and has studied with many Masters from around the world. She is trained in both Western style Feng Shui as well as the traditional Feng Shui methods of Flying Star and 8 Mansions. Helen studied other modalities including Reiki Healing, Chinese Face Reading, Four

Pillars Astrology, and Dowsing. She is also a skilled and accurate Tarot Reader.

For almost a decade, Helen has helped people from all walks of life including celebrities, students, married couples and single women wanting a relationship. Her business, Full Bloom Feng Shui, was established in 2005, at which time she left the corporate world to run her Feng Shui business. Her corporate experience is invaluable when she is consulting with her corporate clients. Helen currently resides in the Los Angeles area.

For more information about Helen or to inquire about her Feng Shui Consulting services, visit her website: www.FullBloomFengShui.com *We Heal Homes*

Notes

Notes

Notes